KITES

BY

Malcolm McPhun

ILLUSTRATED BY

Ed Carr

MACDONALD

First published 1979

Macdonald Educational Ltd
Holywell House
Worship Street
London EC2A 2EN

ISBN 0 356 06325 9 (paperback)
ISBN 0 356 06365 8 (hardback)

Printed by New Interlitho,
Milan, Italy

The Publishers would like to thank
Colin Renwick of the Kite & Balloon
Company for his help in the
preparation of this book.

About this book

This book has been carefully planned to help you become an expert. Look for the special pages to find the information you need. **RECOGNITION** pages, with a **bright blue flash** in the top right-hand corner, contain all the essential information to know and remember. **PROJECT** pages, with a **grey border,** suggest some interesting ideas for things to do and make. At the end of the book there is a useful **REFERENCE** section.

The fun of kites

Kites have been flown for thousands of years. If you have already flown one you'll know why. It's a wonderful feeling when you launch your kite successfully and see it fluttering and dancing high up in the sky above you.

Building and designing kites
But there is more to enjoying kites than just flying them. It is also fun to build your own kite. In the book you will find details of classic kite patterns you can build yourself.

You can also build a kite to your own design, using materials you have bought from a kite shop or simply things you have found around the house. Old newspapers and sheets, brown wrapping paper and plastic bags, even your jacket, can all be put to good use, as you will see.

It's a good idea to stick your name and address on your kite. Then if it's blown away or gets stuck in a tree, it can always be returned to you.

Kites in company
Kite flying is becoming increasingly popular – so you don't have to fly your kite alone. You can take part in games and competitions by joining a kite club or association. The reference section at the back of the book will give you more details. If there isn't a club in your area, why not form your own?

◄ **Flying a kite is a good way of making new friends.**

The parts of a kite

All kites have the same basic structure. The frame, spine and spars form the main body of the kite. They are covered by the sail. The kite is controlled by the bridle and the main flying line. Many kites also have a tail and a keel, to help stabilize them.

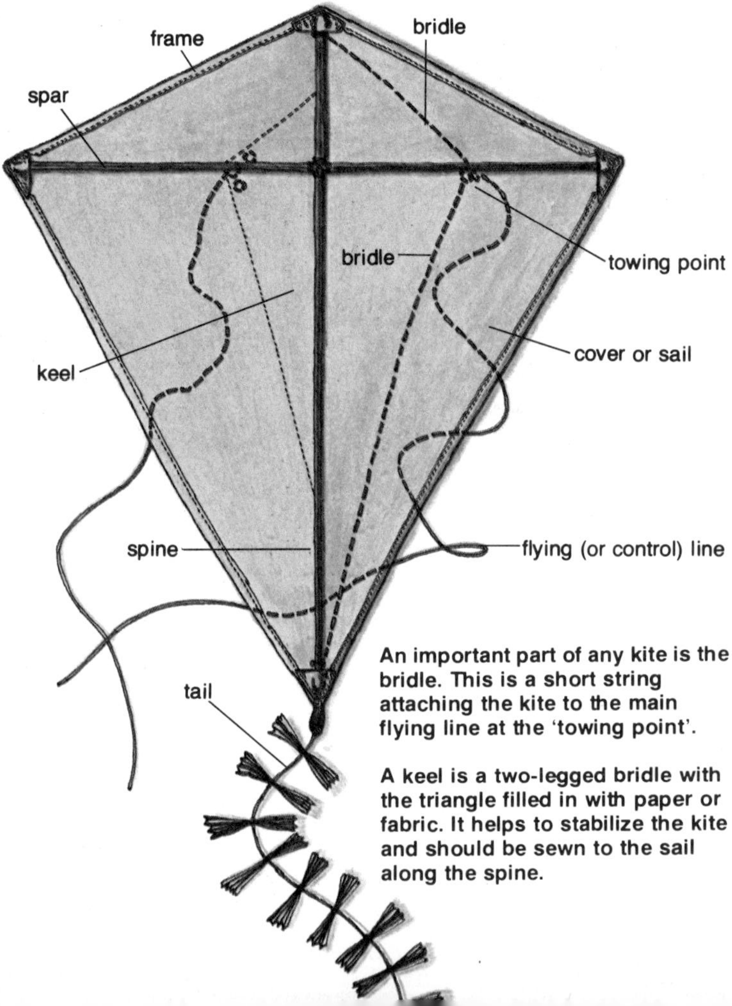

An important part of any kite is the bridle. This is a short string attaching the kite to the main flying line at the 'towing point'.

A keel is a two-legged bridle with the triangle filled in with paper or fabric. It helps to stabilize the kite and should be sewn to the sail along the spine.

Different types of kite

Basic patterns
Although there are thousands of different kites, they can be divided into three main groups: flat, bowed and box.

Most kites are a variation of one of these three types. Some of the best-known variations are the **compound kite** (like the box but with wings), the **sled,** the **delta,** and the **parafoil** (which relies solely on the pressure of the wind to give it shape).

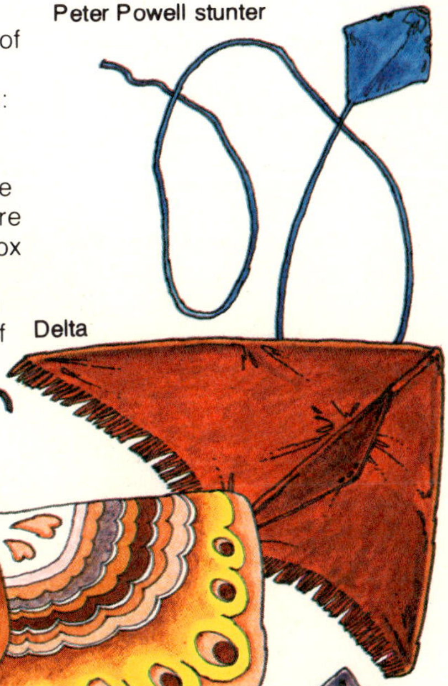

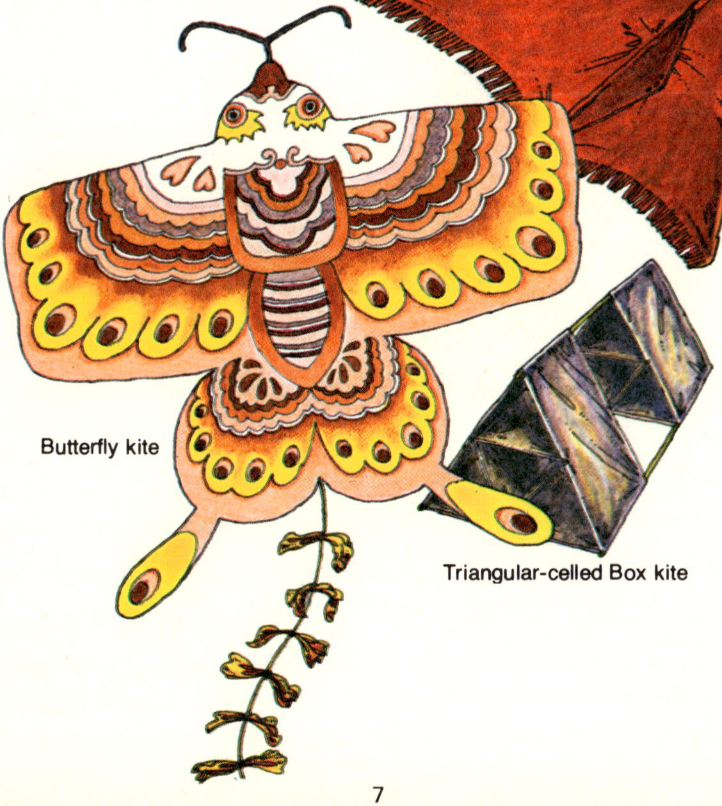

More kites

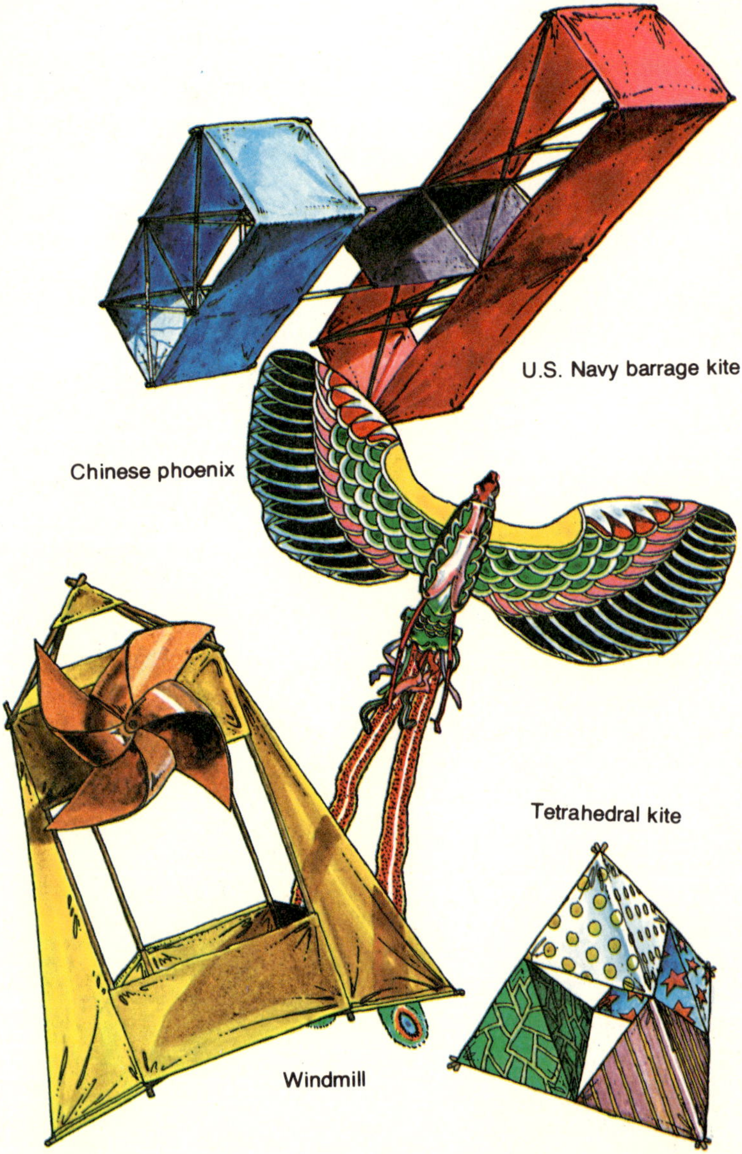
U.S. Navy barrage kite
Chinese phoenix
Tetrahedral kite
Windmill

Some forms of kite have changed very little since they were first invented. The **box, tetrahedral** and **flexifoil** are all fairly recent inventions but the shapes of these Chinese, Indian and Japanese kites have been the same for centuries.

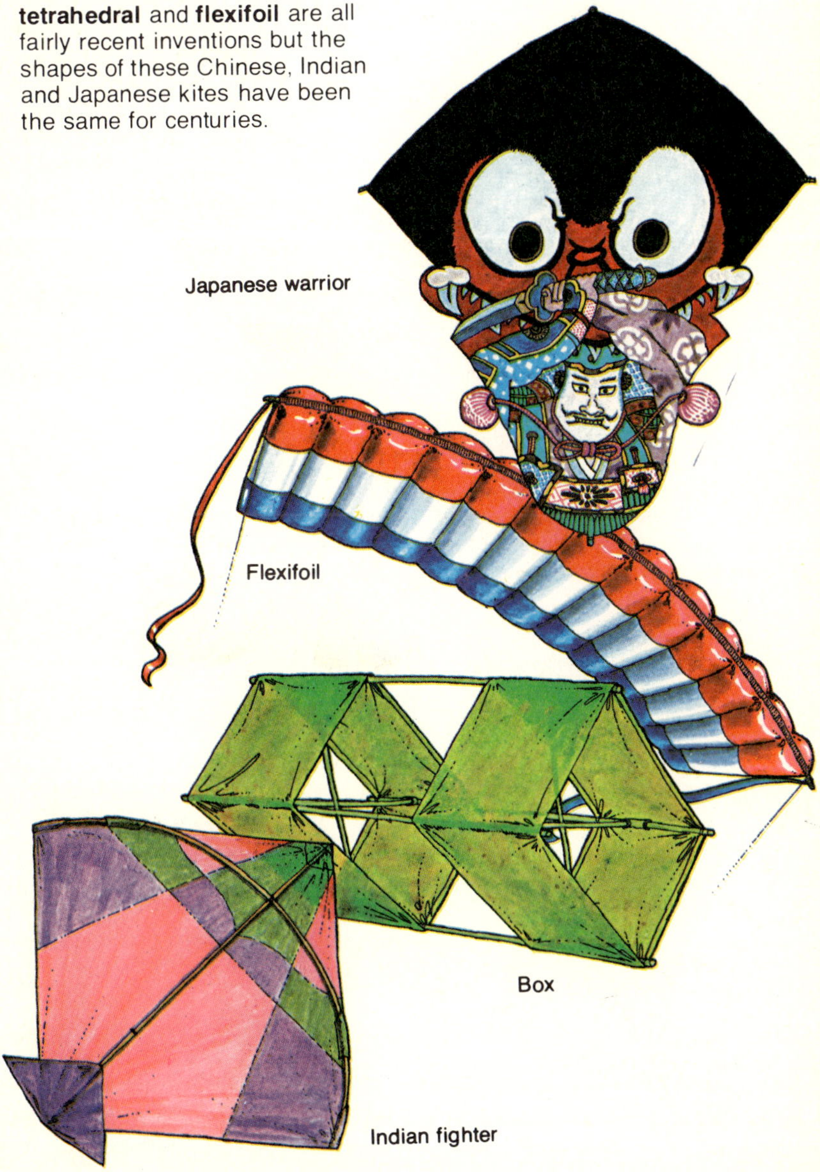

How kites fly

Aerofoils

A kite, like an aeroplane, is heavier than air. In order for it to get off the ground, an upward force has to be produced by the wind.

The shape of an aeroplane wing is called an 'aerofoil'. The wing is lifted upwards because the air travelling over the top of its curved surface has to go faster than the air passing underneath. Fast-moving air creates less pressure; this means there is more pressure underneath the wing, and this helps to force it upwards.

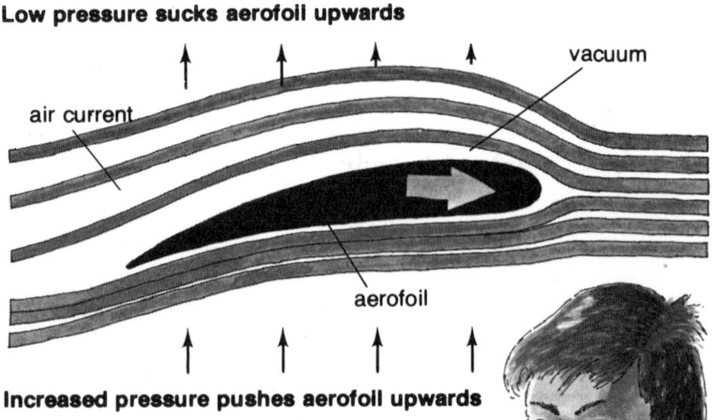

Test for yourself how an aerofoil works.

Bend a strip of card to the slight curved shape of an aerofoil. Fold the end over so that it will hang on a pencil. Blow steadily over the top of the card and it will move upwards into a level position.

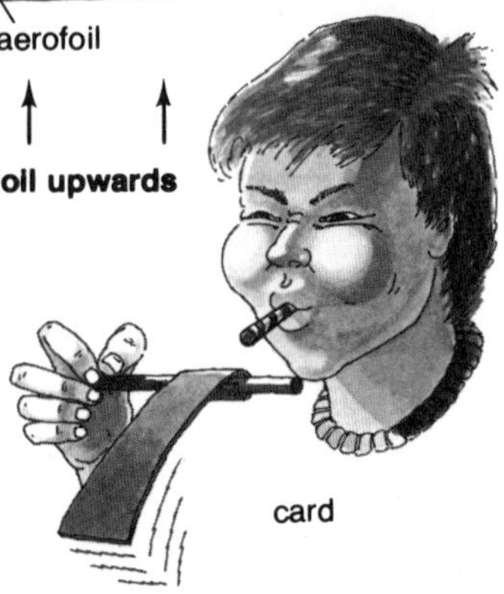

The angle of attack

Some kites have curved surfaces and behave in the same way as aerofoils. Others have flat surfaces that are set at an angle (the angle of attack).

An aeroplane at such a steep angle would stall because the airflow over it would break up into turbulence. But a kite is stable enough to be held in this position by its bridle and control line, and lift continues to be produced.

The effect of the wind

The strength or speed of the wind also affects how well a kite flies. Some kites need only light breezes to make them fly; other, heavier kites need fairly strong winds.

But you can make some kites (like the Classic Diamond shown below) fly in a variety of wind conditions. This is done by adjusting the position of the bridle to alter the kite's angle of attack. This means that you increase or decrease the amount of sail surface that catches the wind.

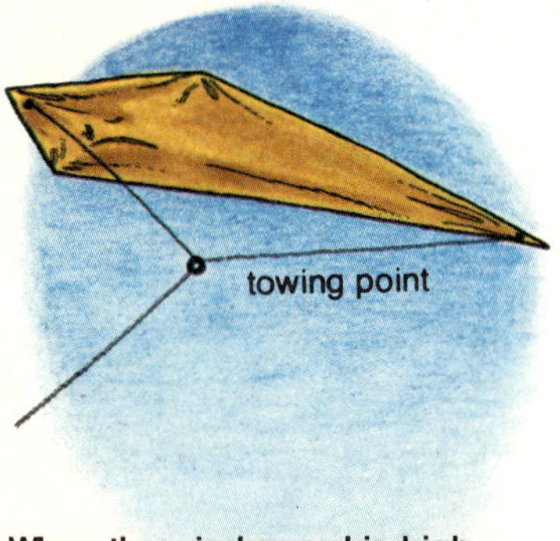

When the wind speed is high, move the towing point towards the front of the kite. This will create a low angle of attack, presenting less of the sail to catch the wind.

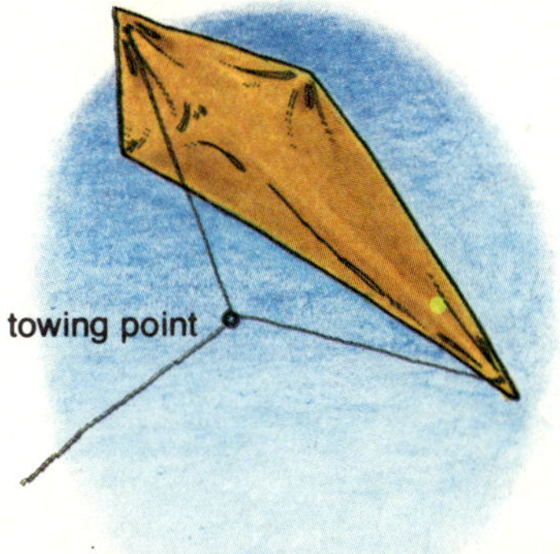

In light breezes, attach the control line closer to the rear of the kite. This will create a high angle of attack, increasing the amount of sail surface presented to the wind.

Where to fly your kite

As any kite flyer will tell you, your first kite will always be the most important one. But do think carefully about where you are going to launch it from.

Kites will fly just about anywhere. All they need is a slight breeze. But if you choose the wrong launching site, it is all too easy to lose your kite.

The right site

The best places to fly kites are large, open spaces: parks and public playing fields in towns; beaches, commons and grassy fields in the country.

A good launching site should also be open to the wind and well away from trees, tall buildings and electric power lines.

One of the best places to launch a kite is on a beach, especially if there are sand dunes. The wind blowing over the dunes provides upward currents of air that will take your kite up quickly and easily, and there is plenty of space to run about in.

▼ Launching a kite on the beach.

The correct way to fly your kite is to stand with your back to the wind.

◄ A flat field is a better place than a hill for launching your kite.

▼ The top of a hill, like tall trees and buildings, causes the wind to move about in lots of different directions. This is called 'turbulence'.

Turbulence builds up on the downwind slope of a hill. So if you are in a hilly area, launch your kite on the windward side, about 25 metres or so below the top. You will find, too, that the updraught will help your kite to gain height.

DO'S and DON'TS OF KITE FLYING

☐ DO fly safely: avoid people and animals
☐ DO wear gloves
☐ DO choose an open area to fly your kite in – never within 5km of an airfield
☐ DO work out a signal system with your helper – it will make launching much easier
☐ DON'T fly near overhead cables or pylons
☐ DON'T leave old bits of line where you've been flying
☐ DON'T fly your kite too high – the legal limit is 60 metres
☐ DON'T fly too near other kites
☐ DON'T fly in a thunderstorm – your kite could act as a lightning conductor

SOME KITE RECORDS

The **largest** kite ever flown was made of 3,100 panes of paper and weighed 8½ tons.

The **greatest number** of kites to be flown in train: 1.050; the top kite reached 2,000 metres.

The **highest** a kite has ever reached: 9,000 metres.

The **longest time** a kite has been flown: 169 hours.

Launching a kite

A single-handed launch.

Preparations for launching

Before you launch your kite, make sure that its balance is correct. Let out a little line and throw the kite into the air. If it hangs down on one side, however slightly, correct the balance by pressing a small piece of plasticine onto the other side.

Adjust the bridle according to the speed of the wind. An elastic bridle (*see page 34*) is useful in a strong wind as it allows the kite to lie flatter. Finally, check all knots for tightness.

Launching on your own

If your kite has a tail, lay it out towards you in line with the direction of the wind. Then stand almost sideways to the breeze. Hold your kite at arm's length and away from the direction of the wind. Then raise your arm gently.

If there is not enough wind, ask a friend to help you launch the kite.

The wind will catch the sail and lift the kite from your hand. Slowly pay out line; the stronger the wind speed, the faster the kite will rise.

Launching with a friend

If there isn't enough wind at ground level for a single-handed launch, ask a friend to help you. He should hold the kite downwind about 50 metres away.

Place the reel on the ground and hold the line taut. When you signal, your helper should raise the kite in both hands so that it catches the wind.

As soon as your friend lets go of the kite, haul in the line. As the kite gains height, tug at the line to give it the extra lift it needs to reach a steady breeze. Very soon all the line taken in at the launch will be used up and your kite will be flying directly from the reel.

Controlling a kite

Box kites and bowed kites
Launch box and bowed kites from the ground. Place the box facing the wind then pull gently on the line so that it tilts forward and catches the breeze. Put the bowed kite face-down, holding the line loosely. Its curved front will catch the wind and lift off the ground.

Once your kite is in the air, it needs plenty of attention to keep it going where you want it to.

Winching

Use this method of raising your kite when the wind speed is low and your kite starts to lose height immediately after launching.

Let the line go slack so that the kite starts to fall to the ground. Then quickly take in the line until the sail catches the wind and flies up again.

Allow the kite to sink once more by letting out extra line. Then, again, reel in the line very quickly to make the kite climb.

Keep on repeating these movements until your kite has gained enough height to catch a strong enough breeze to keep it aloft.

The kite should keep on taking line from the reel as it needs it. But if it won't go any higher than 15m or so, the wind is probably too light and you will have to winch the kite up (*see opposite*).

Remember, the higher your kite flies, the longer it will take to correct any errors. Watch out, too, for other kite flyers; kites can be seriously damaged if they collide.

Coping with a nose-dive

If your kite is a fast climber, in a strong wind it may rise directly above your head and then go into a dive. Stop it from crashing by letting out plenty of line. It will then float gently to the ground.

Another way of dealing with this problem is to make the kite 'loop the loop'. Let go suddenly of 5 metres or so of line. The kite will dip to one side and circle. Then quickly take up the slack line. The kite will move upwards in a different direction until it reaches its zenith (or highest point).

By repeating this movement, you will be able to make your kite dance in the sky.

Bowed kites

Kites with bowed spars are often the most stable in strong winds. A bow is like the dihedral, or upward curve, of an aeroplane wing. When the bow tilts to one side, the pressure increases on the other and pushes it back to a level position.

The top picture shows what a bowed kite looks like when flying steadily in strong winds. But the kite in the bottom picture has climbed too fast. It has gone over the top and into a nose-dive.

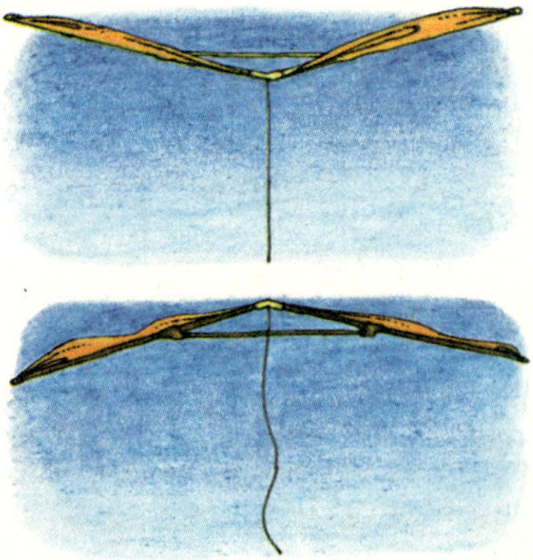

Bringing a kite down

Skilled kite-flyers can land their kites exactly where they want without damaging the kite.

Winding in the slack
Begin your landing by winding in the slack at a steady rate. If you are flying single-handed, place the reel on the ground and hold the line. Then pull it in hand over hand. Be sure to wear gloves.

In a strong breeze, it is easier to do this by walking towards your kite. Keep the line steady, paying it out a little to avoid breaking it if the kite is pulling too strongly. By this method it is possible to get the kite to come directly into your hand without it once touching the ground – a very stylish landing.

In light breezes, bring your kite to within a few feet of the ground, then let go of the line completely. Your kite will float gently downwards.

Remember, never pull your kite along the ground once it has landed – this may damage it.

Always fly your kite well away from trees. If it does get stuck in one, make sure the tree is safe to climb before you attempt to retrieve it.

Otherwise cut the line at the highest point you can reach and the wind may blow the kite down for you. If your name and address are on it, it can be returned if it is found.

Always wear gloves when you fly a kite: the line will burn your hands badly if you don't. Thin leather gloves are best. But any type of glove is better than bare hands.

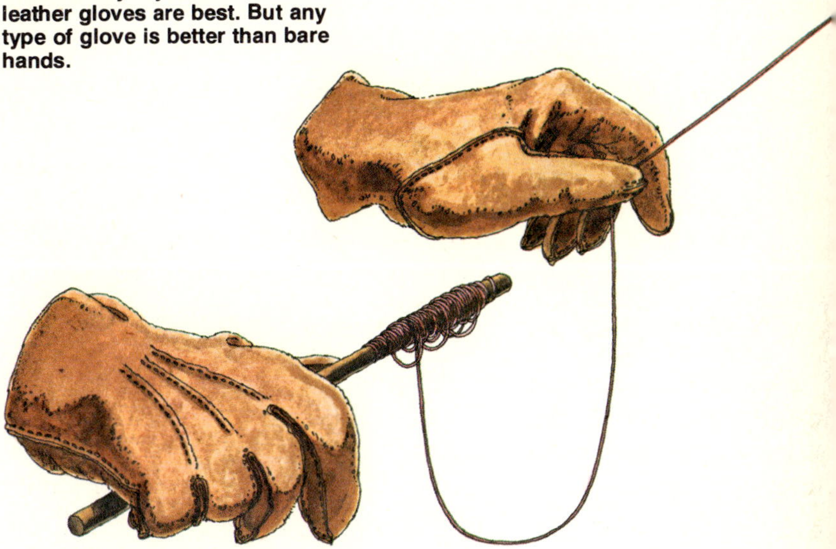

Landing in the wind

In strong winds, a helper can make all the difference to achieving a safe landing.

Walk towards the kite, pulling the line down as you do so. You may find it easier if you place a piece of strong fabric over the line and pull on that.

When you are about 50 metres away from your helper, stop and hold the line, taking the tension off it while he walks towards you reeling it in. Keep on doing this until the kite is directly above. Then haul it down, making sure it doesn't loop or side-slip.

* * *

These are the only safe ways to land your kite. They avoid the strain on the line, and lower the chances of the line breaking and of you losing your kite.

Building your own kite

Your work area

You will need plenty of space in which to work. Your working surface should be large enough for you to lay out all your tools and materials. If necessary, protect it with layers of newspaper or a polythene sheet.

In the summer you can always build your kite outside. But make sure you choose somewhere that is sheltered from the wind.

When attaching a paper sail to the frame, glue on paper pockets to cover the ends of the spar and spine.

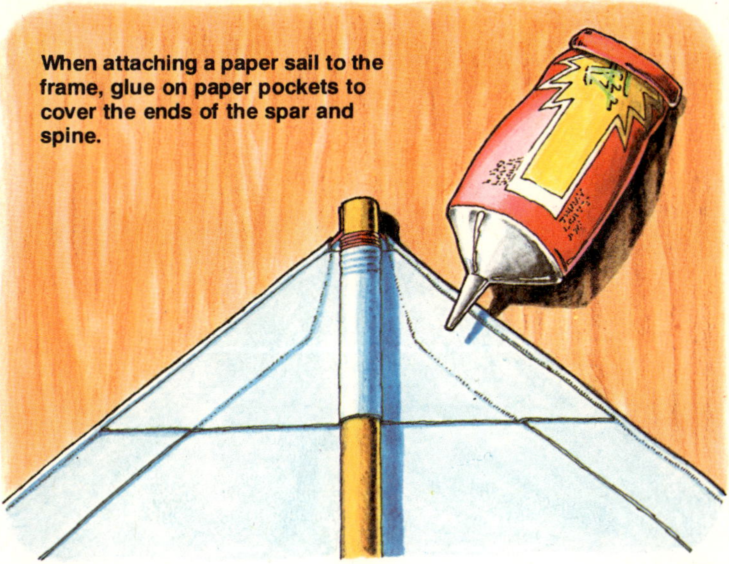

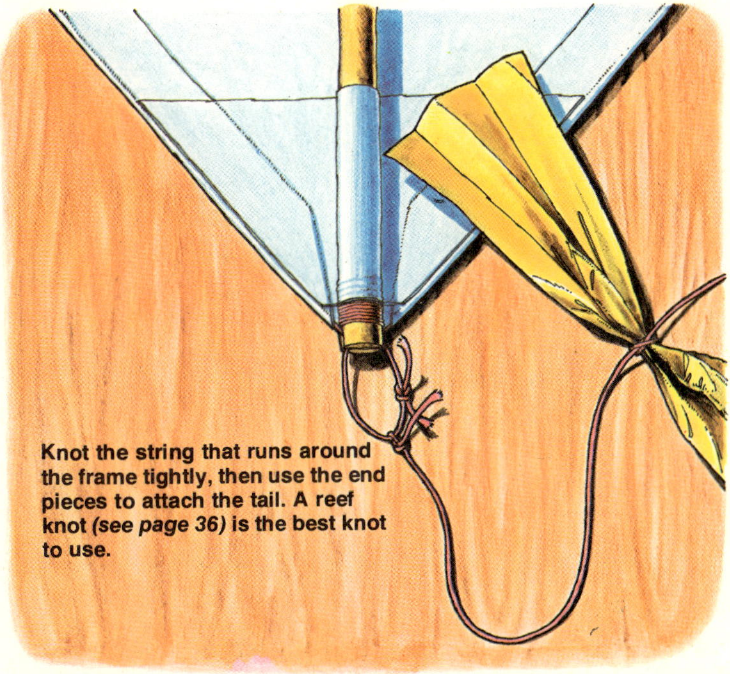

Knot the string that runs around the frame tightly, then use the end pieces to attach the tail. A reef knot *(see page 36)* is the best knot to use.

The tools you will need

All the tools you need for making your own kite are shown on these two pages. Most of them are easily available.

It's a good idea to take scissors, glue and sellotape with you when you fly your kite, just in case you have to make any instant repairs.

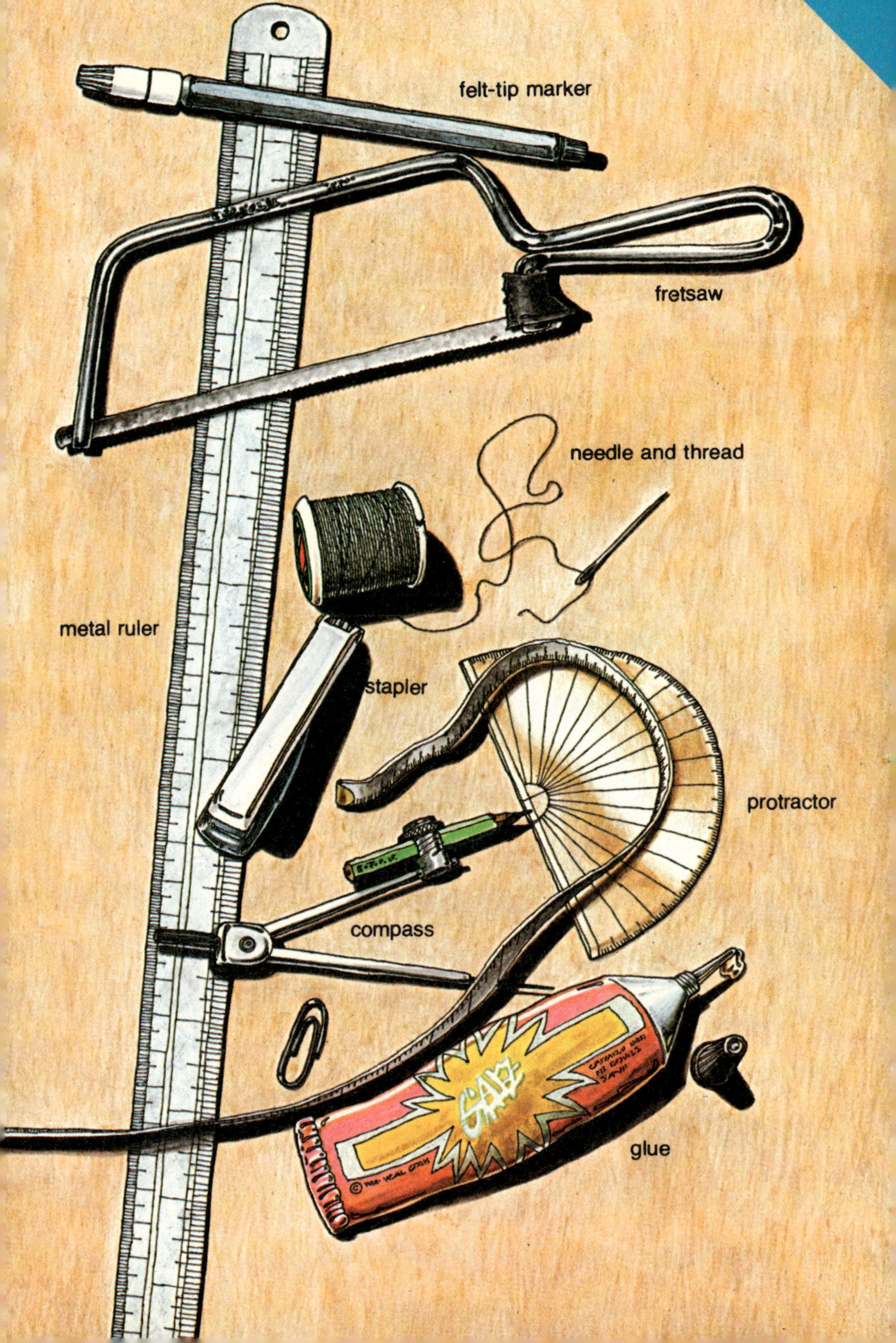
felt-tip marker
fretsaw
needle and thread
metal ruler
stapler
protractor
compass
glue

Making the frame

Materials

You can make your frame from a variety of materials: wood dowel, light aluminium tubing, plastic tubing, fibreglass rods or bamboo. The simplest frame to make is the cross. Wood dowel is the best material to use for this.

Curved frames

Bamboo is very good for making a curved frame. But be careful to get the balance right. If you use bamboo with another wood, make sure that they are exactly the same thickness and strength. Test the spars for balance before you assemble them. Mark the centre of the spar, then balance it on the edge of a knife. If one side is heavier, even it up with sandpaper.

Making the cross piece

Lash the spine and spar together with strong line or string. Then secure the ends by painting them with quick-drying glue.

Make small notches about ½cm deep at each end of both the spar and the spine. These will hold the string that runs around the edge of the kite. Lash well to prevent splitting.

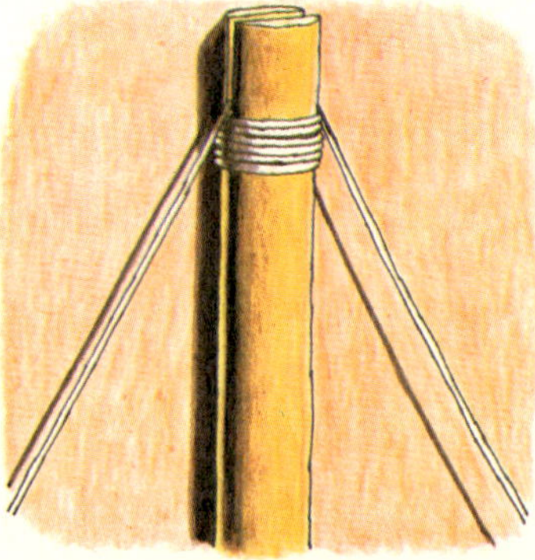

Bamboo

Split bamboo into lengths by placing a thin-bladed knife, like a penknife, at one end of the bamboo and tapping it with a hammer. The bamboo will split into two equal halves. By using the same method, you can quarter each half or split the bamboo into eighths.

How to bend and splice bamboo

Soak the bamboo pieces in water until they soften. They can then be formed to the shape you want. Tie the ends together with a piece of line if you want to make a bow. Adjust the string so that the curved bamboo fits the shape of your kite.

For more complex shapes, bend the bamboo and then pin it to a board and leave it to dry. When dry your bamboo pieces will retain their new shape.

You can also use this method of soaking and bending with unsplit bamboo and wood dowel. But remember that both these will need much longer soaking – both before and after they have been tied into shape.

Cutting bamboo

Always use a fretsaw when cutting bamboo across its width.

Use a knife to split bamboo along its length. Sandpaper it afterwards for a smooth finish and the proper balance.

Paper kites

Materials
Use the lightest materials you can find. Coloured tissue paper, wrapping paper and even old newspaper make good sails. Use thin dowel or bamboo for the frame. You will also need string and strong glue.

Style of kite
A paper kite can be made up in almost any shape. Illustrated below is the Classic Diamond. Make the cross as shown on page 24. Remember to test each piece for balance and strength.

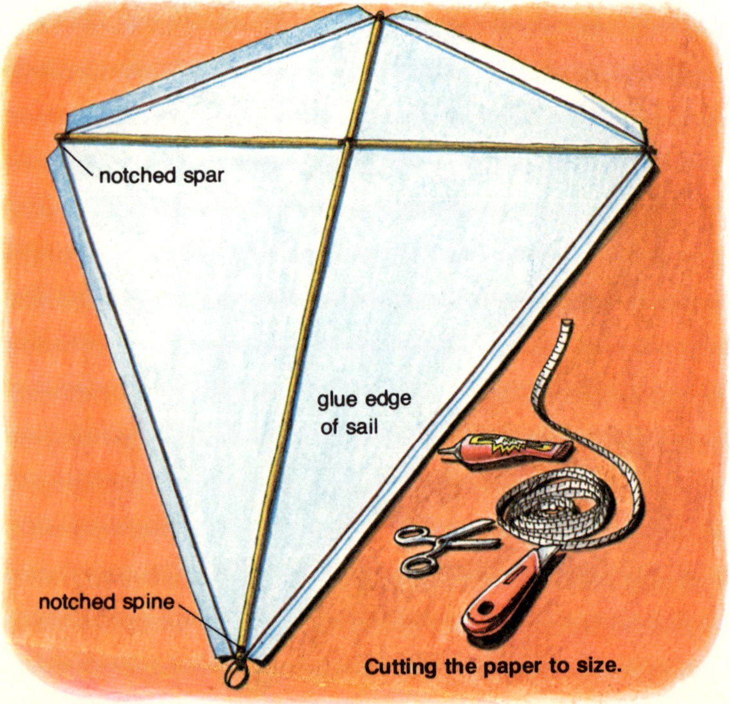

Cutting the paper to size.

Attaching the sail

Make the diamond shape with strong string. Pass it around the notched ends of the spine and spar, keeping it as tight as possible while you tie the end into a loop. Use this loop for attaching the tail later.

Lay the frame over a sheet of paper and cut it to shape, as shown opposite, with a margin all around the edge. Glue the edges and fold over. Strengthen by adding extra strips of glued paper over the folds. Clothes pegs will help to hold the edges in place until they are dry.

A paper kite can be decorated in lots of different ways. There are some suggestions on page 28. Giving the sail a coat of aeroplane dope will help to stiffen and strengthen it.

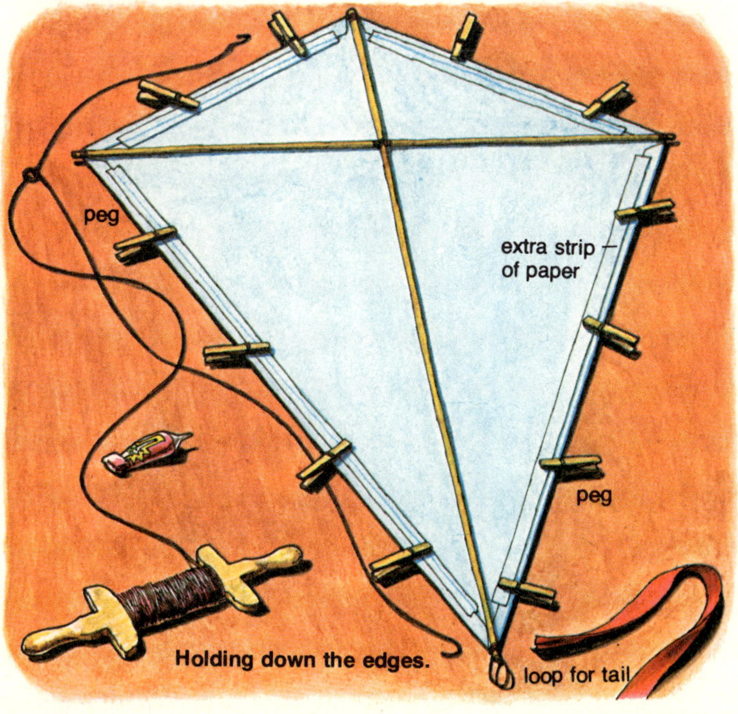

Holding down the edges.

Ideas for decorating your kite

Paper kites are the easiest to decorate. You can paint faces, designs or flags onto the sail, advertise your name or your football team, or embarrass your friends! The possibilities are endless. The only thing you need to remember is to use bright colours and a bold design: it will have to stand out at a distance.

Ed

Cloth kites

Materials

A cloth sail is heavier than a paper one, so it is better suited to larger kite designs. Silk is one of the best materials to use but is very expensive. Cotton and nylon – such as tyvek and rip-stop – are cheaper, but make sure that they are of a very fine-weave or they will not be properly wind resistant.

Cutting to shape

Start by cutting out a paper pattern in the shape of the kite you want to make. Pin it to the cloth and cut round it, leaving a margin of about 1½cm beyond the edge of the pattern. Pinking shears that leave a zigzag pattern are best for this.

Fold over the cut edges and sew up the hem. The hem should be about 3cm wide. Leave a gap for the string to thread over the notches in the spar and spine.

Hold both the pattern and the cloth in place with heavy weights such as bricks.

If you have pinking shears, use them to cut your material. They leave a zigzag edge which prevents fraying.

Fitting the sail

The finished sail, when hemmed, should be about 1½cm smaller all round than the frame. Sew cloth tapes a few centimetres long to each corner. They will help to keep the sail in place.

Starting at the bottom, thread the string for the frame through the hem, looping it over the notches as you go. Pull the cord tight then tie it securely.

Use the tapes to pull the sail very tight over the frame, then secure them with sticky tape or string.

Some kites may need 'pockets' to hold the ends of the spine and spars. You can make these from scraps of cloth just wide enough to take the sticks. Sew them to the appropriate places on the sail.

Remember, always attach sails to the front of the kite so that the hems will face away from the wind.

Use a zigzag stitch to sew up the hem.

Kite tails

Making a tail

You can make kite tails out of newspaper, crêpe paper, thin card, fabric or ribbon.

Experiment with different lengths. A rough guide is to make the tail 7 times as long as the spine of the kite.

The tail should sway gently in the opposite direction to the kite. If it flutters about or the kite spins in the air, your tail is too short.

If the kite won't take off, then the tail is too long and heavy.

Tail designs

The tails illustrated here are all easy to make – why not experiment with several?

☐ **Traditional bow** – made out of paper or cloth.

☐ **Streamers** – made from crêpe or tissue paper. There should be the same number on each side.

☐ **Fabric tail** – stitch a tape down the centre of short pieces of material.

☐ **Ribbon tail** – use two long lengths of ribbon.

☐ **Loop** – attach the ribbon to your kite at both ends.

☐ **Handkerchief** – tie lengths of material to one long strip.

☐ **Ladder** – made from thin card, good for high winds.

☐ **Drogue** – one of the most efficient forms of tail. Remove the bottom from a paper cup. Use several in a high wind.

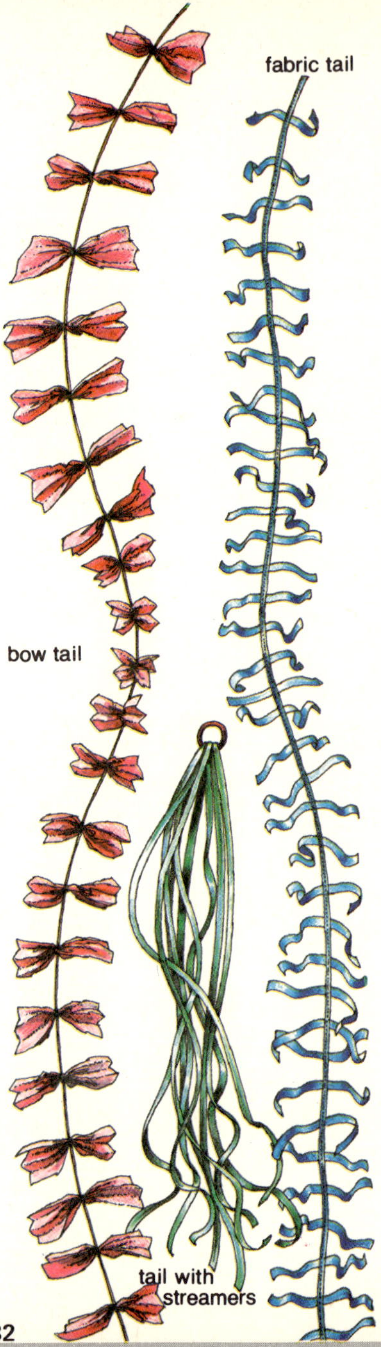

At high altitudes, your kite may be tossed about by strong winds. You can stabilize most types by adding a tail.

A tail creates 'drag', helping the kite to stay face on to the wind as well as making it look more attractive.

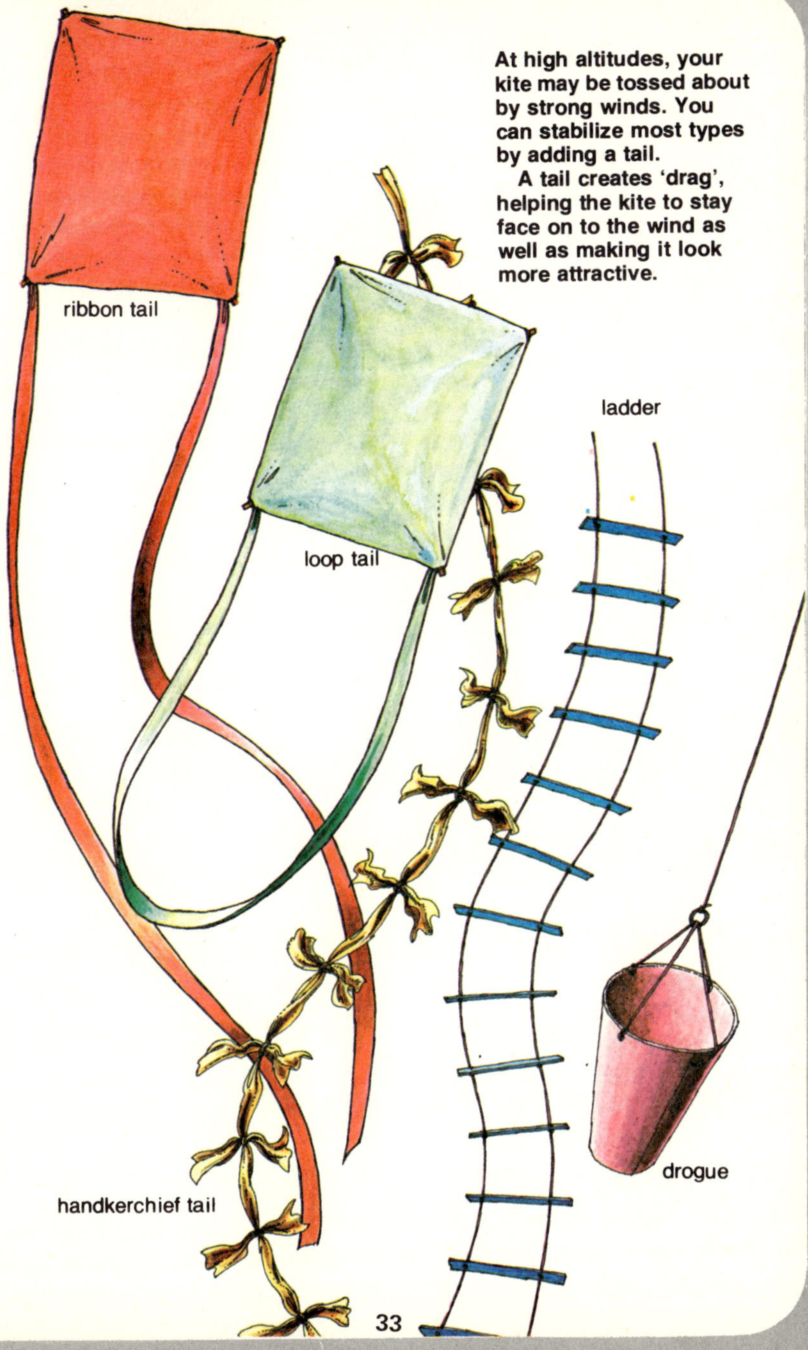

Bridles and lines

A bridle is used to attach a kite to the flying, or 'control', line. You can make a bridle out of strong string, cord or plaited nylon. It can have a number of short strings or 'legs'. These come together at the towing point, where they are attached to the control line by a strong metal ring (the towing ring).

Position of the towing point
The towing point should be about **one-third** of the way down the spine; and the distance from it to the sail should be **half** the length of the spine.

The control line
Choosing a control line depends on the size of your kite and the wind speed. Use silk or cotton thread for very light kites; strong string or cord, or nylon line, for heavier models.

You will need at least 60 metres of line, with a breaking strain of about 4.5kg for small kites, and up to 45kg for heavier kites. If you use string, wax it with a candle to cut down its wind resistance.

An elastic bridle like this allows your kite to adjust automatically to different wind speeds.

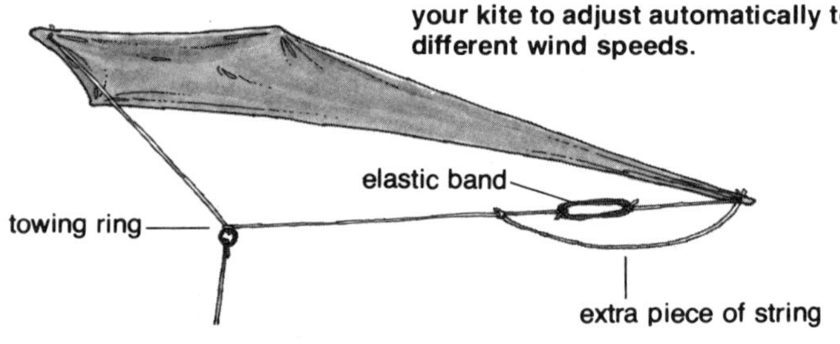

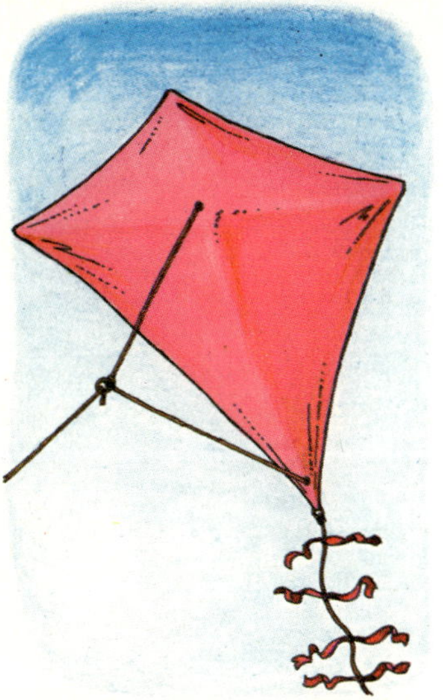

▲ Attach a bridle with two legs near the bottom of the spine and to the centre of the cross-spar.

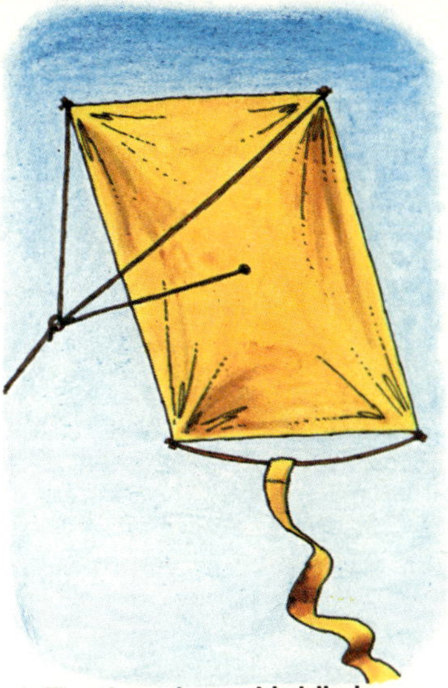

▲ The three-legged bridle is attached at the centre, top-right and top-left.

▲ The four-legged bridle is attached mid-way along each spar. The bottom lines are the longest.

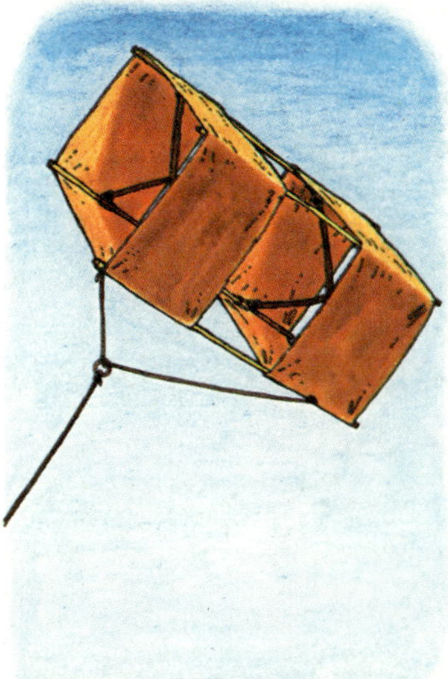

▲ On a box kite the bridle should be positioned on one side only, as illustrated above. The rear line is the longest one.

Useful knots for kite flying

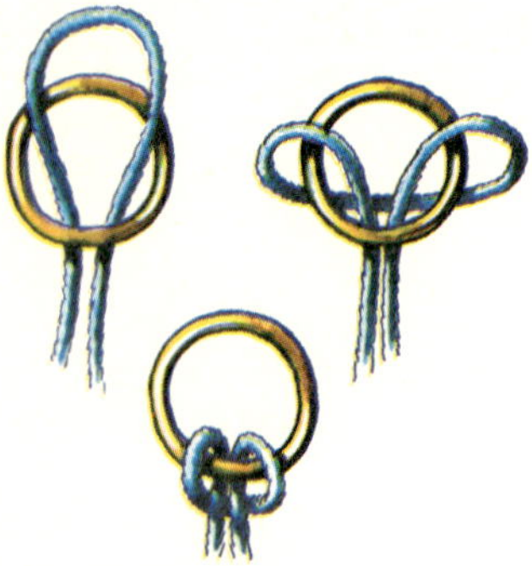

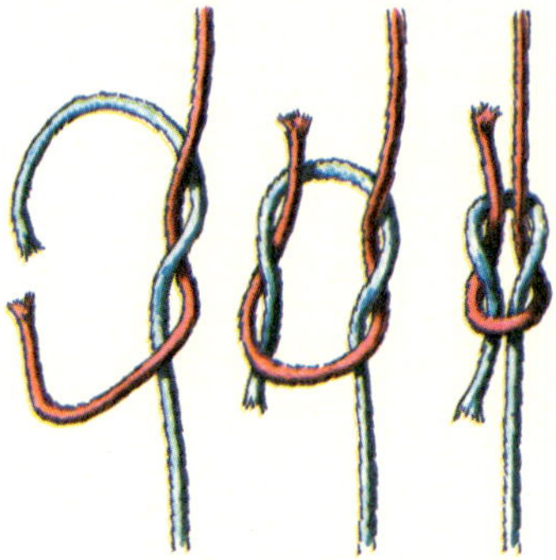

▲ **Lark's head hitch:** use for securing the towing ring to the bridle and for attaching other kites to the line for flying in trains.

▲ **Reef knot:** useful knot for finishing off ends and attaching lengths of line. Remember to pass left over right then right over left.

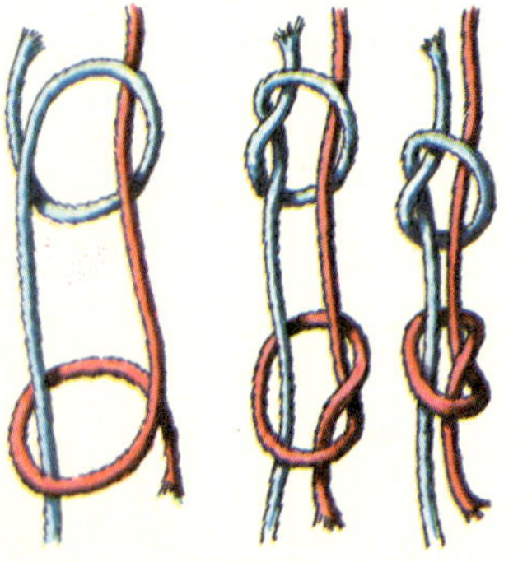

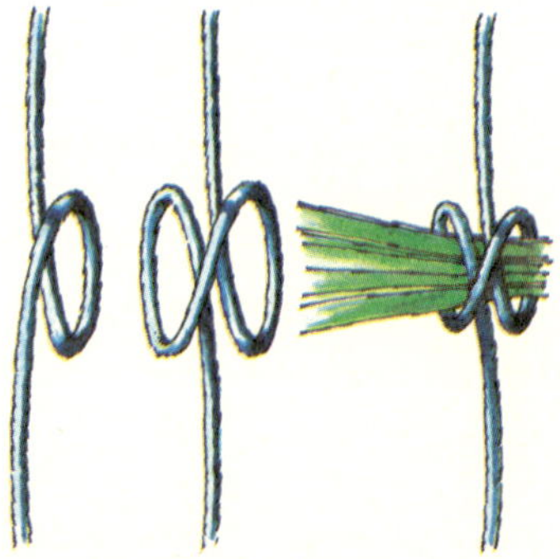

▲ **Fisherman's knot:** very good knot for joining two lengths of string together, especially when the lines are of different thicknesses.

▲ **Clove hitch:** has the advantage of not needing the whole length of string pulled through. Good for tying on bows to the tail.

Reels

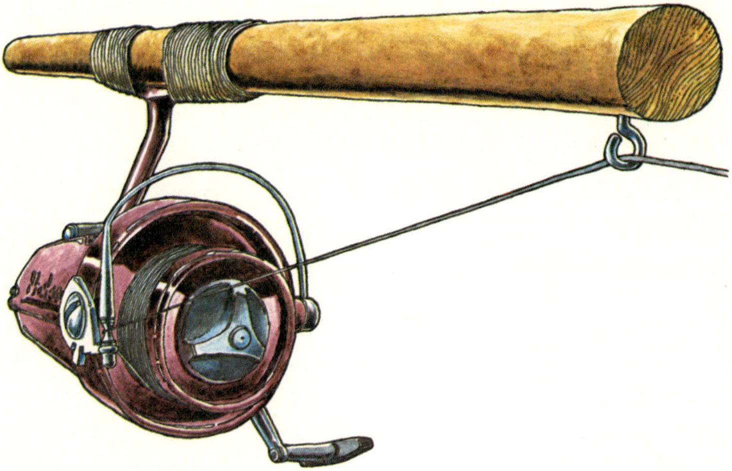

Fishing rod and reel

The simplest reel of all is just a piece of wood or a strong, straight stick around which you can wind your line. But if you are flying at high altitudes, you will find that winding in such long lengths of line is very tiring. It's much more fun to have a proper reel.

A fishing reel

For small to medium-weight kites, try using a fishing rod and reel. Make sure that the reel will take enough line to allow you to fly your kite at heights of up to 60 metres. But only use a reel that you can handle comfortably – if the reel is too heavy, it will be just as tiring as using a piece of wood.

Making your own reel is not difficult – and is much cheaper than buying a fishing reel. See the next page for some ideas.

Making your own reel

You can easily make any of the reels illustrated below out of plywood or an old plank.

Materials: sharp knife; fretsaw; drill and bit; and plenty of sandpaper.

1. This bobbin is the simplest of all to make. Mark the design on a piece of wood with a crayon and cut it out with a fretsaw. Carve it into shape with a sharp knife. The slit at the end is to hold the end of the line fast.

It is very important to round off all the edges to avoid fraying your line. Smooth down the wood with sandpaper.

2. Make this bobbin in the same way as number **1.** The handles at each end make winding easier.

3. You will need to use lengths of 2cm dowel for this reel.

Drill the holes in the flat pieces and push the dowel through. Leave enough sticking out on each side to form handles. Secure all the joints with strong glue.

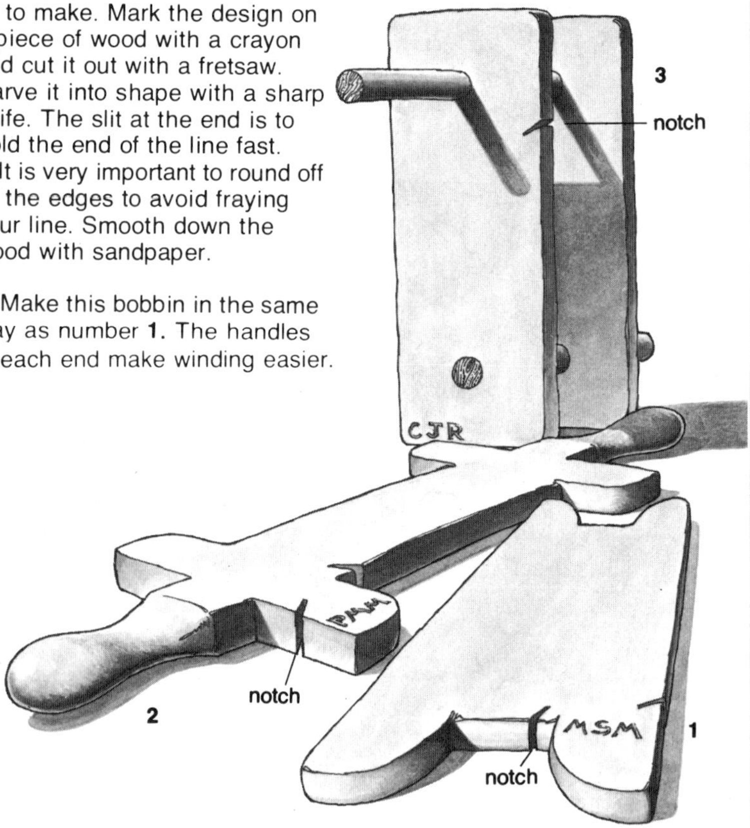

Famous kite designs

On the following pages you will find out how to make the kites illustrated below.

Some designs include a scale, so that you can make the kite any size you like. Measure each part against the scale.

The number you read off can be used in cms or inches, or multiplied by 2 or 5, depending on the size of kite you want.

Use the measurements given for the other kites; they fly best when made to this size.

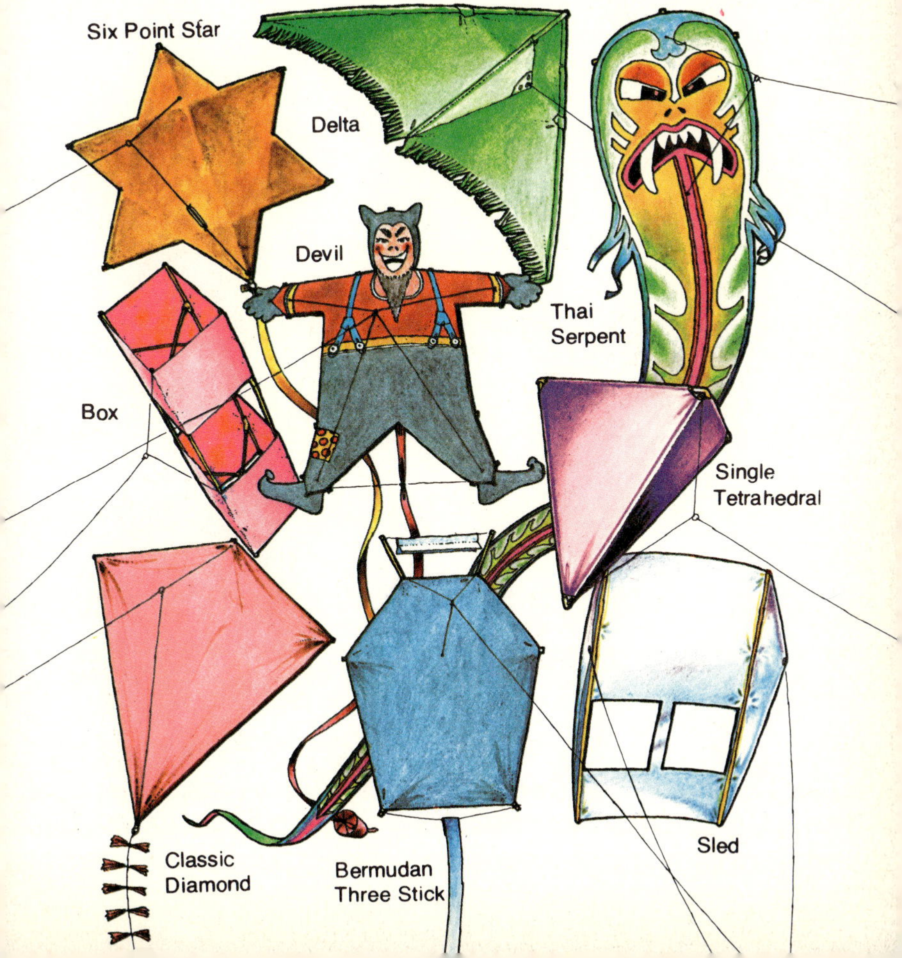

Classic Diamond

Specifications
Sail: paper or cloth.
Frame: dowel.
Bridle: two-legged.
Tail: paper bows.
Fly in light to moderate winds.

Construction details
Glue pockets on to a paper sail to cover the spar and spine ends.

If using cloth, follow the instructions given for cloth kites on pages 30–31.

It is also quite easy to make variations of this basic kite. You can experiment by bowing the spar, or by adding central fins or a keel to increase its stability.

Detail: pocket covering end of spine.

Detail: lashing on cross-spar.

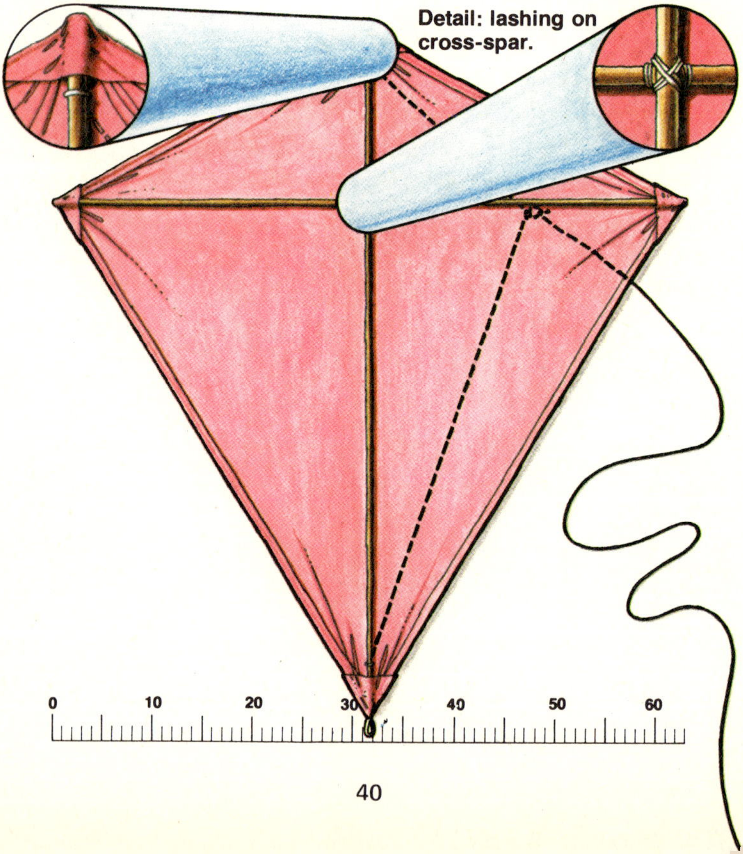

Delta

Specifications
Sail: cloth, plastic, nylon or tyvek.
Spine and spar: dowel.
Bridle: keel.
Fly in light to gentle winds.

Construction details
1. Lay the spine down the middle of the sail. Then fold the material over and sew along the spine, sewing in the keel at the same time.
2. Hem the edge of the sail over the two lengths of dowel.
3. Double-stitch small pockets to hold the cross-spar.
4. Make holes in the keel for attaching the flying line.

Detail: pocket holding cross-spar.

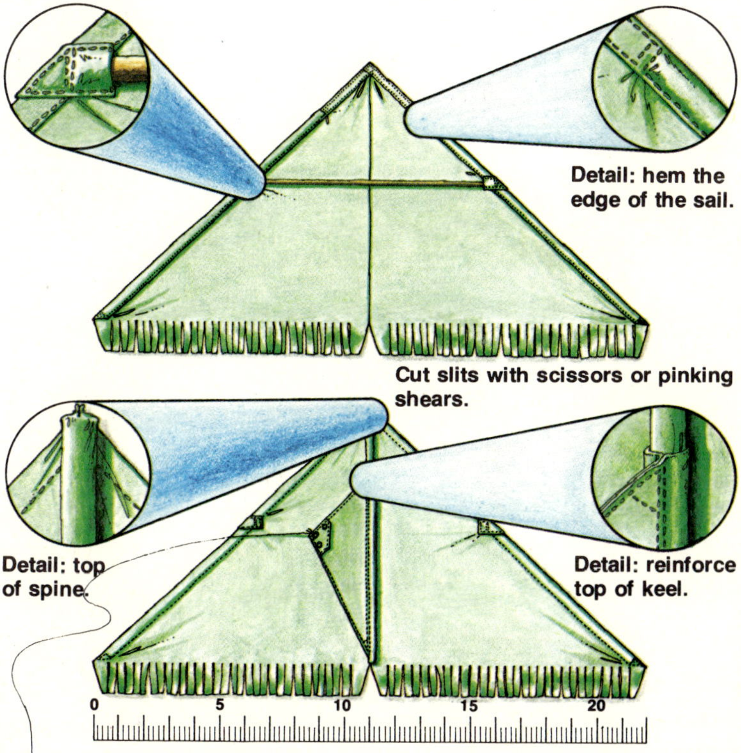

Devil kite

Specifications
Sail: strong paper.
Frame: bamboo.
Bridle: four-legged.
Tail: up to 5 metres of ribbon with a drogue at the end.
A good flyer in steady winds.

Construction details
Draw half the devil outline below on to a piece of paper with 5cm squares ruled on it. Cut out the pattern and lay it on the sail paper.

Draw round it, then turn it over and make the other half of the outline. Use string for the frame and strengthen the head with a piece of wire. Fold over the edges of the sail and glue.

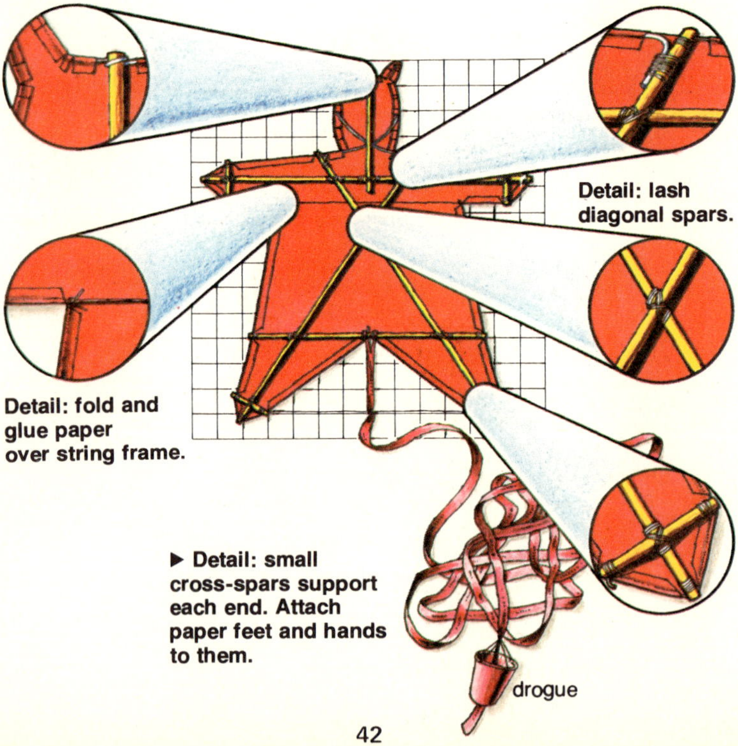

Single Tetrahedral

Specifications
Sail: plastic sheet.
Frame: dowel.
Bridle: two-legged.
No tail.
Fly in moderate to strong breezes.

Construction details
Cut six pieces of dowel 75cm long. Make an equilateral triangle using three dowels. Use plastic tubing for the joints, as shown below.

Build a pyramid with the remaining dowels, again joined with plastic tubing, and attach the sail to two sides of it. Use more tape to strengthen the edges facing the bridle.

Detail: join spars with plastic tubing.

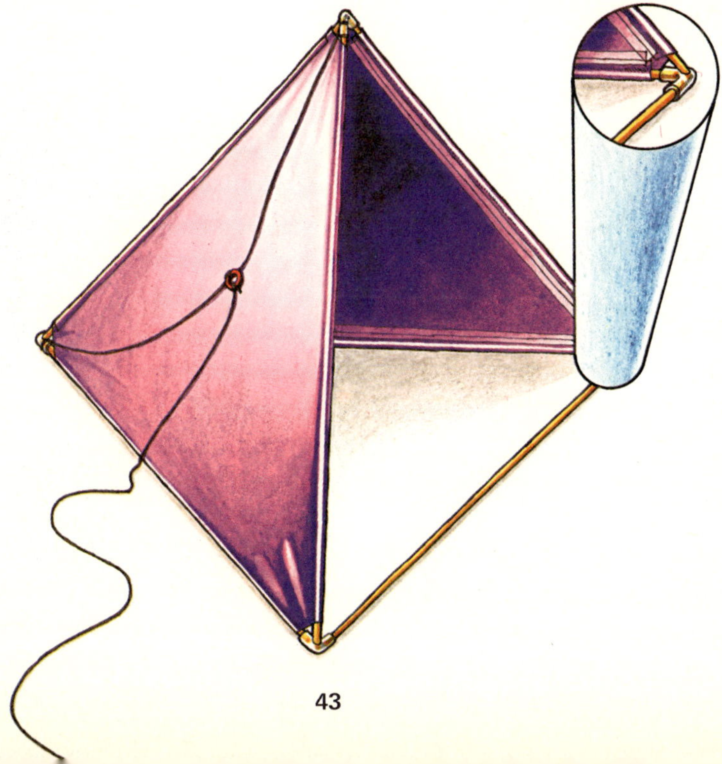

Sled

Specifications
Sail: tinfoil, plastic or tyvek.
Spines: dowel.
Bridle: two-legged.
No tail.
The cut-out vents give the sled greater than average stability in a wide range of wind speeds.

Construction details
One of the easiest kites to make. Cut out the sail. Attach the two spines with sticky tape. Strengthen the bridling points with tape, then punch holes for the bridling lines. The bridle should be longer than for most kites: approximately twice the length of the spine.

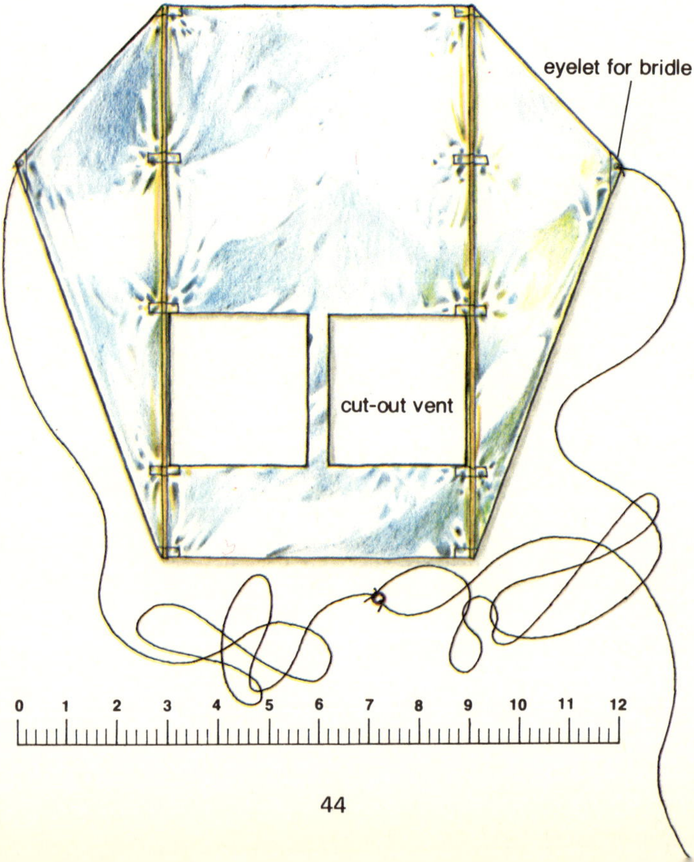

Six Point Star

Specifications
Sail: paper.
Frame: split bamboo and string.
Bridle: two-legged (you can also use an elastic bridle).
Tail: paper streamers or bows.

Construction details
Lightly glue the frame to a sheet of paper. Cut round the star shape, leaving enough paper to make flaps. Fold the flaps over the frame and glue.

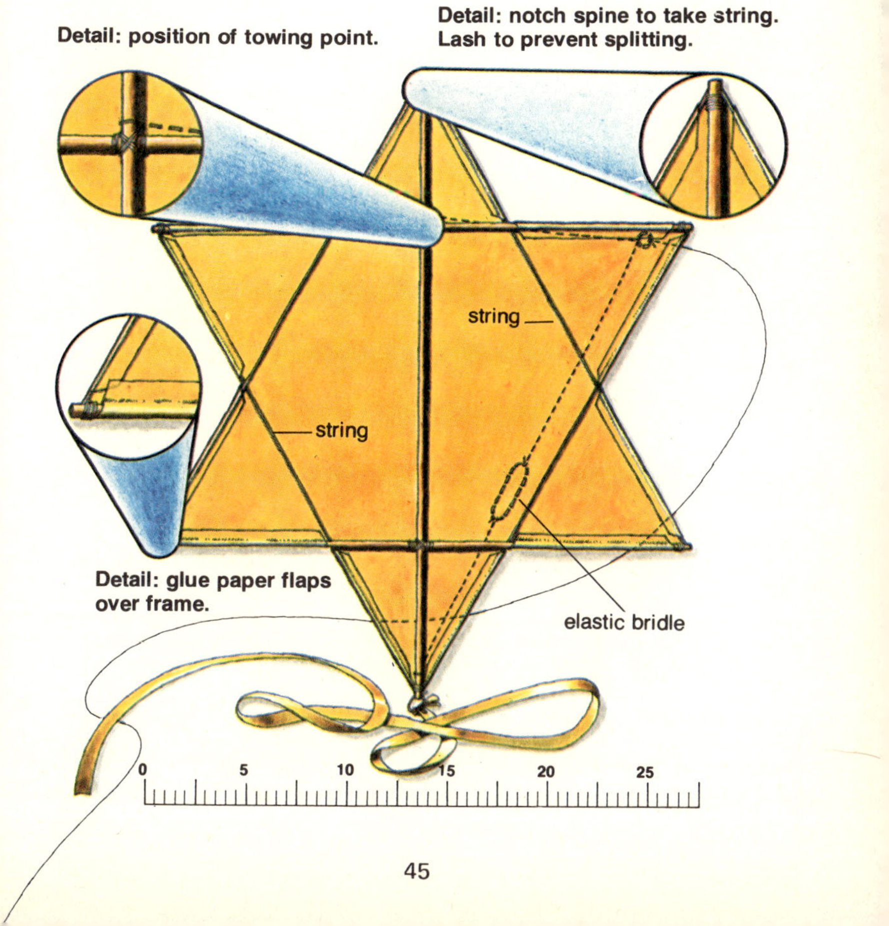

Thai Serpent

Specifications
Sail: silk, paper, thin plastic or tyvek.
Frame: split bamboo.
Tail: the longer the better.
Bridle: two-legged.
Fly in light to moderate winds.

Construction details
The tail should be strengthened along the middle with sticky tape or a piece of fabric or ribbon.

Split and then bend the bamboo frame to shape as described on page 25.

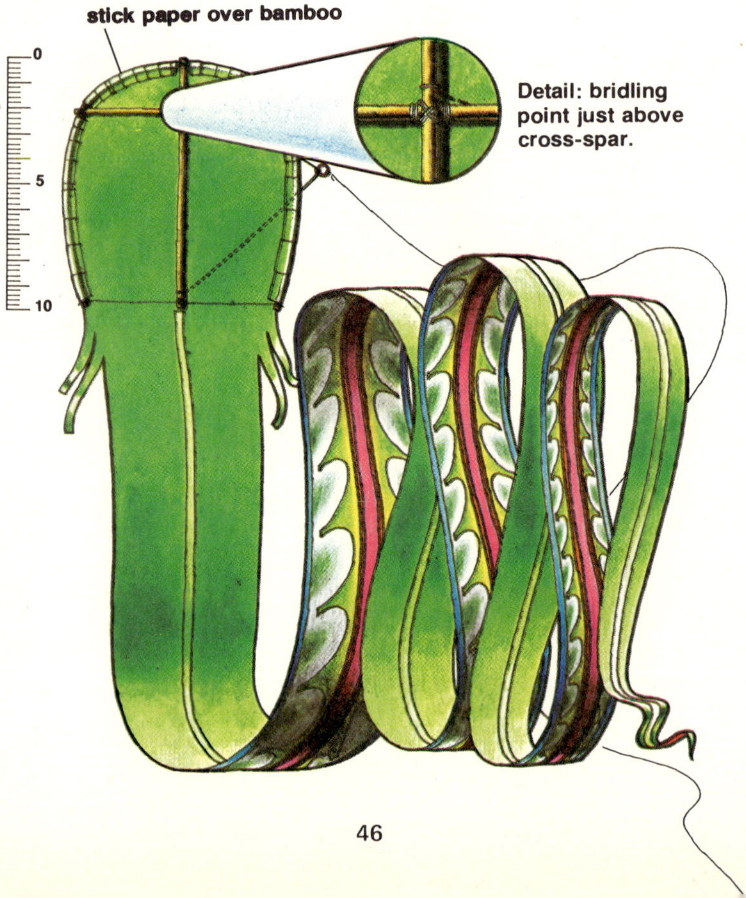

Bermudan Three Stick

Specifications
Sail: strong tissue or wrapping paper.
Frame: split bamboo or thin dowel and string.
Tail: paper streamer or light ribbon.
Bridle: three-legged.

Construction details
The string around the edge should be quite fine or the kite will be too heavy. Stick the paper flaps over it.

The kite can be fitted with a hummer, or even tethered and left to fly by itself.

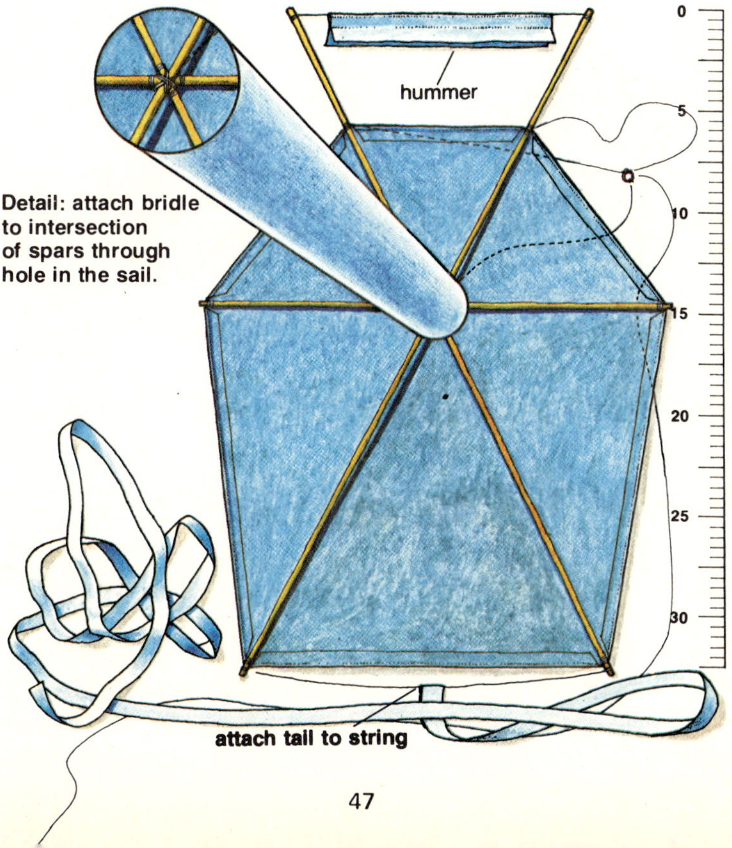

Box kite

Specifications
Sail: rip-stop nylon, tyvek or fine-weave cotton.
Frame: dowel; four spars × 90cm long, and four × 43cm long.
Bridle: two-legged.
No tail.
Fly in moderate to strong winds.
Can be flown tethered.

Construction details
The sail should fit as tightly as possible.

The diagonal cross-sticks should fit very closely against the horizontal spars, so make them a little longer than the space they have to cross.

Remove the cross-sticks to make the kite collapsible.

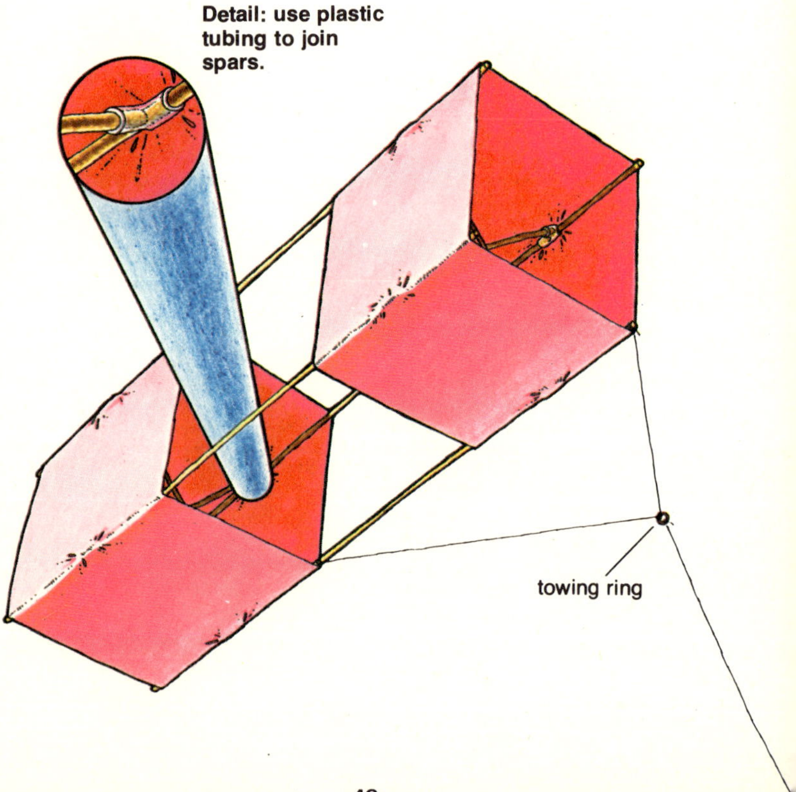

Indoor kites

If it is too windy to fly your kite outside, why not try making one of these tiny indoor kites?

A mini Classic Diamond

Use very thin balsa wood for the frame, and silk or cotton thread for the outline around spine and spar. To make the sail use either of these methods:

1. Add a drop of glycerine to aeroplane dope and pour the mixture onto a dish of cold water. Carefully slide the frame under the mixture with a pair of tweezers and lift it upwards. Allow to dry, then fix on the bridle with tiny specks of glue.
2. Make the sail out of very fine plastic film or cellophane. Fix it to the frame with dots of glue.

A stamp kite

The bridle and line should be of the finest silk thread. Attach them by simply dampening the glue on the back of the stamp.

You can fly the kites in a draught, or in the stream of air from a hairdryer.

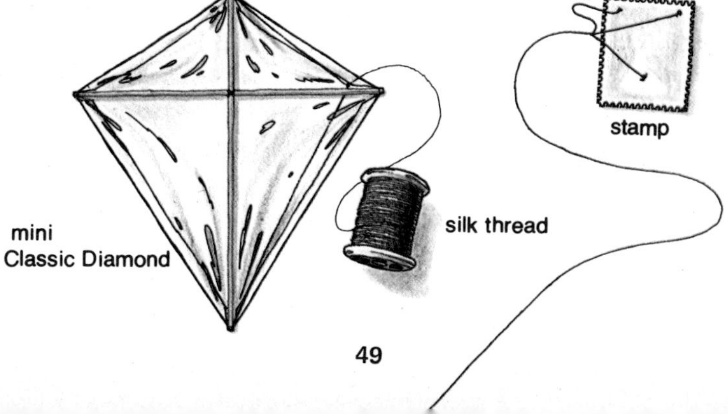

Designing your own kite

If you have made kites successfully from the patterns in this book, you may want to design your own.

Combining shapes
Remember that all kites are made up of the same basic forms. You can combine different shapes, like the ones illustrated opposite, to make some very unusual kites.

As you experiment with different forms you may even discover an entirely new type of kite. The **flexifoil**, which looks like a flying airbed, the **parafoil**, which is similar to a parachute, and the popular **stunter** kite, are all recent inventions.

Turn your jacket into a dual-control kite by using curved bamboo for the spars and string for the frame.

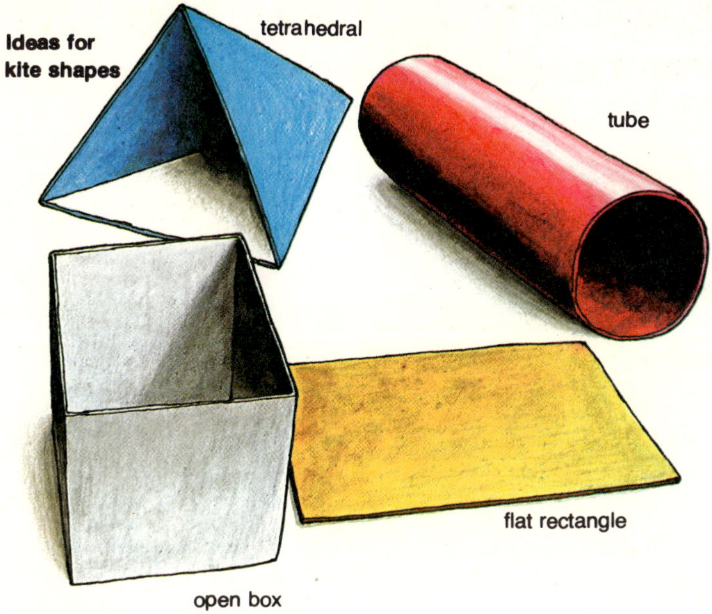

Useful hints for kite-making

☐ **1.** Check that each part is perfectly balanced.
☐ **2.** Always lash notched spars to prevent splitting.
☐ **3.** Lash intersections evenly, then paint with strong glue to make them waterproof.
☐ **4.** Strengthen bridle-holes with extra pieces of paper or cloth.
☐ **5.** Use a swivel-clip to attach the main flying line to the towing ring.
☐ **6.** Leave a 3cm margin around the edge of the sail for turning over to glue or stitch the hem.
☐ **7.** Stick string outlines to the sail with pieces of sticky tape to make your kite more streamlined.
☐ **8.** Finally, to avoid unnecessary crashes, always experiment with your bridling and check for balance before launching a new kite.

Windsocks and banners, messengers and flags

Messengers

Messengers are great fun. They fly up the control line and release small objects such as parachutes or gliders.

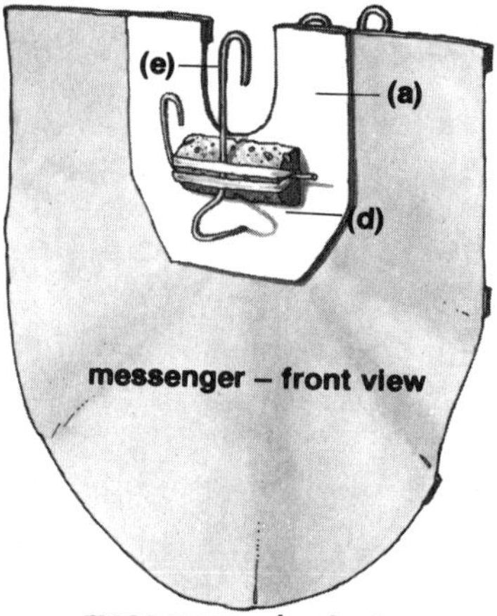

messenger – back view

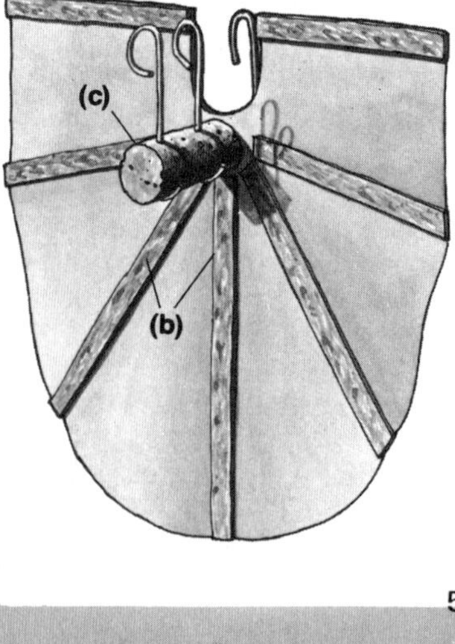

Making a messenger

Cut a piece of paper to the shape illustrated on the left. Strengthen it at the top with a piece of card **(a)**.

Reinforce the other side with small bamboo or balsa wood sticks **(b)**. Then glue on a cork with two straightened-out paper clips stuck into the top **(c)**.

Cut another cork in half and force a straightened paper clip through the middle of it. Loop an elastic band round each end **(d)**. Glue it to the card.

Slip another straightened paper clip through the elastic band **(e)**. Hang your parachute or glider on the loop at the bottom.

A release mechanism

Tie a small piece of wood to the line near the towing point with a clove-hitch (see page 36). This will act as a 'stop' for the messenger.

The messenger in action

Now launch your kite. When it is flying well, send the messenger up by looping the paper clips over the control line and then letting go.

When the messenger reaches the stop, the hanger will spring back and release its load. The messenger will then slide back down the line, ready for reloading.

Flags

These are easy to make, but should only be flown by stable kites. Stiffen the edge nearest the line with a length of bamboo.

Banners

Stiffen the ends of the banner with bamboo. Launch two kites and when they are both at equal heights, attach the banner to their control lines.

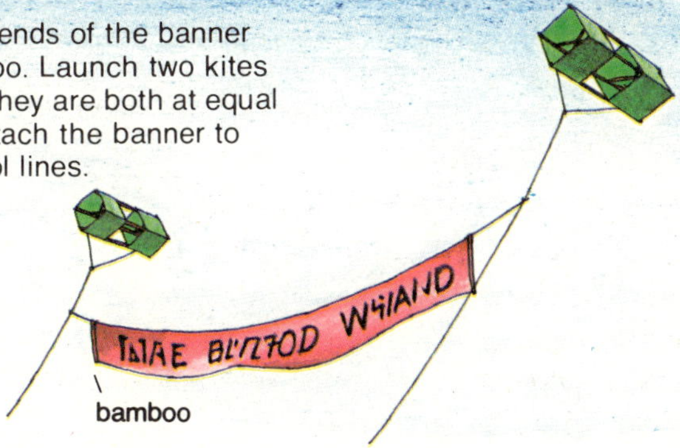

A windsock

Make the two hoops out of stiff wire. Attach them to a tube made of closely-woven cloth or plastic. With cloth, turn the ends over each hoop and hem. With plastic, use strong glue.

Kite games

Flying a kite need not be a solitary hobby. If you have a friend who also enjoys kite flying, you could try some of these kite games.

Scarecrow. If you live in the country, you could use hummers on your kites to scare away birds from the crops. In a steady breeze you can even tether your kite and collect it later.

Dancing kites. Some kites can be made to dance in the sky. A group of you could try flying your kites in time to music; you could even put on a display.

Water races. Use your kites to pull small logs or model boats along the water. Fasten them to the control line with a short piece of line and a metal ring.

Hummer: attach a string across the top of two spar ends. Make sure it is as taut as possible. Fold and glue a strip of stiff paper over the string – it will make a loud buzzing sound.

Paper tail chopping: tie a long paper streamer to each kite. The point of the game is to see which of you can first chop through the other person's tail with their line.

Dancing kite: make your kite dance, or loop the loop as described on page 17. You will need a lot of practice before you can do it really well.

Kite trains: launch the first kite and when it has reached about 50 metres, attach the second one to the control line with a strong metal ring. Add further kites at about 25-metre intervals.

Ghost kite: don't overload the kite with a heavy wiring system. Remember to balance the bulbs perfectly if you are using fairy lights. Check your kite for 'lift' first.

Kite trains. Several kites can be flown together on the same line. This is called flying in trains. You can organize a competition to see who can fly the most. Don't be too ambitious – it takes a lot of strength to keep the trains under control.

Ghost kites. Turn your kite into a ghost at night. Choose an evening with enough moonlight to let you see what you are doing, then attach a small torch behind the sail. For a very dramatic effect, decorate the kite with fairy lights connected to a pencil battery. The Devil is a good kite to use for this.

* * *

Remember that different wind conditions will affect the amount of weight your kite can carry.

Kite competitions

Kite festivals and competitions are becoming more and more popular. If you don't belong to a kite-flying club or association, you and your friends could organize your own festival along similar lines.

Classifying kites

Kites are normally divided into three classes for competitions: flat, box and bowed. All the kites flown should be made by the entrants, so that everyone has the same chance of doing well. Choose your programme from the events listed below:

1. *Freestyle:* judged for originality of design, uniqueness of flying style, and variety of stunts and manoeuvres. Flying time should be agreed beforehand.

Try to think of ways to involve onlookers. Why not invite someone in the crowd to hold your control line or help with launching? But remember, it's not their fault if something goes wrong!

2. *Most beautiful kite:* judged for colour, originality of design, construction and flying performance.

3. *Highest flying kite:* all kites should be flown on a maximum of 60m of flying line, and given a two-minute period to gain height.

4. *Longest distance flyer:* the kite that travels furthest from the flying-line marker in a two-minute period after launching.

5. *Smallest kite in flight:* all kites should be held on a minimum line length of 8m and fly over the heads of the contestants. The kites must have frames and are allowed tails or stabilizers.

6. *Largest kite in flight:* the flying line should have a breaking strain of at least 40kg. Kites must be airborne and flying at the full 60m within an agreed period of time.

Reference section

Booklist

If you have enjoyed this book, you will probably want to find out more about making and flying kites.

Some of the books below were published in the United States. So if you can't find them in a bookshop, why not ask your local library to order them for you.

How to Make and Fly Kites by Barwell and Bailey (Studio Vista)

Colourful Kites from Japan by Tadao Saito (Ward Lock)

Flying Kites by James Wagenvoord (Macmillan, New York)

The Penguin Book of Kites by David Pelham (Penguin Books)

25 Kites That Fly by Leslie Hunt (Dover Publications, New York)

Making and Flying Kites by Lloyd, Mitchell and Thomas (Beaver Books)

Kites by Jean-Paul Mouvier (Collins)

Kites by Ron Moulton (Pelham Books)

Kite Craft by Lee Scott Newman (Allen and Unwin)

Kite Making and Flying by Harold Ridgway (Arco, Mayflower)

Kites, an Historical Survey by Clive Hart (Faber)

Your Book of Kites by Clive Hart (Faber)

World on a String: the Story of Kites by J. Yolen (World Publishing Company, New York)

Kite Cookery by Don Dunford (Cochranes, Oxford)

Kites by Ben White (E. J. Arnold, Scimitar Series)

Kitefolio by Timothy Burkhart (Double Elephant, Berkley and Wildwood House)

Fun With Kites by John and Kate Dyson (Angus and Robertson)

Glossary

Aerofoil: a surface specially curved to make the air flowing across it provide lift.

Banner: a long rectangle, usually made of cloth, carrying a simple message.

Beaufort Scale: a method of gauging wind speed by observing conditions on the ground (see p. 62).

Bowstring: the string that secures the curved spar of a bow kite.

Bridle: the line that runs from the kite's sail, and to which the control line is attached.

Cover: the fabric of a kite, covering the frame and designed to catch the air. Also known as the sail. It can be made of paper, cloth, or nylon.

Drag: the resistance of a kite to air movement. It is affected by both the weight of the kite and its surface area.

Drogue: a conical 'cup' open at both ends. It has the same effect on a kite's flying behaviour as the tail.

Frame: the rigid structure of the kite to which the sail or cover is fastened.

Hummer: a device fitted to kites that whirrs and hums in the breeze.

Keel: a triangular fitting on some kites which adds stability in flight.

Kite train: two or more kites flown from the same control line.

Loop: a circular manoeuvre performed by the kite in the sky.

Messenger: a device which is launched up the control line and checked at the top close to the kite. It releases a small glider or parachute when it reaches the check point.

Spar: the horizontal part of a kite frame.

Spine: the vertical part of a kite frame.

Strut: extra pieces of dowel or bamboo which reinforce the frame.

Tail: fabric or paper bows tied on to the line or streamers attached to the bottom of the kite which add to a kite's stability.

Kite associations

Kite flying is a world-wide pastime and there are associations in many different countries.

Even if you are unlikely to visit Australia or Japan, it is worthwhile joining their kite associations. Through their magazines you will learn about events and competitions as well as new developments in kite design.

You will also find news and articles about kites in *Amateur Airsport*.

For details, write to:
The Old Labour Exchange,
Bow Street,
Langport, Somerset.

Where to write

American Kitefliers Association,
7106 Campfield Road,
Baltimore MD 21207.
(Publishes a quarterly journal: *Kite Lines*.)

Australian Kite Association,
c/o Helen Bushell,
Secretary,
10 Elm Grove,
North Kew 3102,
Victoria, Australia.

Kite Fliers Association of Australia,
c/o Ian Perrin,
69 Fisher Street,
Myrtle Bank,
South Australia 5064.

Le Cerf-Volant Club de France,
c/o Jean-Louis Bousset,
President,
17 Rue Lacharriere,
75011 Paris.

British Kite Flying Association,
c/o Ron Moulton,
P.O. Box 35, Bridge Street,
Hemel Hempstead,
Hertfordshire HP1 1EE.

European Kitefliers Group,
c/o A. Darmenia-Gay,
2 Princess Anne Flats,
Ball Street, Paceville,
Malta GC.

Japan Kite Association,
c/o Singo Modego,
President,
Taimeiken, 1 Chrome,
12–10 Nihonbashi,
Chuoku, Tokyo.

Kitefliers of India,
3126 Lal Darwaza Bazaar,
Sita Ram, Delhi 6, India.

Waikato Kite Club,
c/o C. P. Croft,
19 McCracken Avenue,
Hamilton, New Zealand.

Kite shops

Many department stores and toy shops stock kites. But usually the range offered is limited. Shops specializing in kites not only sell many different types of kites, reels and line, but also papers and fabrics for kite sails as well as materials for making frames. They are also useful advice centres.

Wood yards and hardware merchants are good places to look for bamboo, wood dowel, balsa and glues. And you can get special fabrics and strong lines from ships' chandlers.

Green's Kite Centre,
336 Coles Road,
Burnley,
Lancashire

Kite & Balloon Company,
613 Garratt Lane,
London, S.W.18
(Is also a 'kite hospital' for damaged kites.)

Kitecraft,
38 Calvin Road,
Winton,
Bournemouth, BH9 1LN

Kite Stores Limited,
69 Neal Street,
London WC2

Sky Cat,
Trenance Mill,
St. Austell,
Cornwall PL25 5AQ

Manufacturers and Importers

Flexifoil Kite Co.,
52 Tottenham Street,
London W1P 9PG

Frisco's Cut-a-Kites,
3 Queen Caroline Street,
Hammersmith Broadway,
London W.6

JNT Models
(Top Flite Kites),
Long Street,
Easingwold,
Yorkshire

Cochranes of Oxford Ltd.,
(Dunford Kites),
Leafield,
Oxfordshire OX8 2NT

Multiflite,
Victoria Road,
South Shields,
Tyne and Wear

Brookite,
Francis Terrace,
Junction Road,
London N19

Albatross Kites,
Hill End Farm Works,
Tyttenhanger Green,
St. Albans,
Herts

Wind chart

Although there are several devices for measuring wind-speed, the usual method of gauging wind conditions for flying kites is to use an adaptation of Beaufort's Scale.

This was devised around 1805 by Admiral Francis Beaufort of the British Navy to help sailors judge wind conditions at sea.

The scale ranges from **0** (calm) through various breezes, gales, and storms to **12** (hurricane).

Light steady speeds of about 8 to 15 miles an hour are ideal for the average kite.

Wind speeds of up to 20 miles per hour are safe for sturdy kites with good stability and strong lines.

Only very strong kites should be flown in winds of over 24 miles an hour, otherwise you risk losing your kite.

Effects on Land

0 – Smoke rises vertically.
1 – Smoke drift shows wind direction.
2 – Wind felt on face; leaves rustle.
3 – Leaves and small twigs in constant motion.
4 – Dust and loose paper raised; small branches move.
5 – Small trees in leaf begin to sway.
6 – Large branches move; telegraph wires whistle.

Beaufort No.	Term	mph
0	Calm	0
1	Light air	1–3
2	Light breeze	4–7
3	Gentle breeze	8–12
4	Moderate breeze	13–18
5	Fresh breeze	19–24
6	Strong breeze	25–31

Index